DISC

D1108494

ROCKWELL LECTURES
Rice University

Previously published books in
the Rockwell Lecture series

ARCHAEOLOGY, HISTORICAL ANALOGY, AND EARLY BIBLICAL TRADITION

ARCHAEOLOGY «
HISTORICAL ANAL-
OGY « & EARLY BIB-
LICAL TRADITION
WILLIAM F. ALBRIGHT

LOUISIANA STATE UNIVERSITY PRESS · BATON ROUGE

DEDICATED
To Roger T. O'Callaghan, S.J.,
whose tragic decease ended
a brilliant career.

Copyright © 1966 by
Louisiana State University Press

Library of Congress Catalogue Card Number 66-21755

Printed in the United States of America by
Heritage Printers, Inc.

Designed by Robert L. Nance

ACKNOWLEDGMENTS

Iᴛ ɪs ᴀ ᴘʟᴇᴀsᴜʀᴇ ᴛᴏ ᴇxᴘʀᴇss ᴍʏ ᴛʜᴀɴᴋs ᴛᴏ ᴘʀᴏFᴇssᴏʀ Niels C. Nielsen, Jr., and his colleagues at Rice University, who made my stay at Houston so agreeable while I was giving the Rockwell Lectures in January, 1962. It is also a pleasure to thank the Louisiana State University Press for its forebearance while I kept deferring final delivery of my promised manuscript.

I wish also to express my thanks to my research assistants, Dr. C. S. Mann and Dr. Leona G. Running, for their aid in countless ways, which finally made it possible for me to get this and other volumes into shape for publication. Naturally, since the Rockwell Lectures were given four years ago, the text needed to be brought up to date in detail. It is now entirely abreast of my present information and point of view.

Mᴀʀᴄʜ, 1966   Wɪʟʟɪᴀᴍ F. Aʟʙʀɪɢʜᴛ

CONTENTS

ix

ARCHAEOLOGY, HISTORICAL ANALOGY,
AND EARLY BIBLICAL TRADITION

I

The Historical
Interpretation of
Early Hebrew Literature

WHEN WE APPLY ARCHAEOLOGY OR HISTORICAL analogy to a particular area of research, it is important to define the two terms, to consider their limitations as aids to our reconstruction of history, and to confirm their relevance to particular problems under consideration. For historiographic reasons we shall take up historical analogy first.

Until quite recently, modern historical interpretation of early biblical literature had to deal with events which took place in a vacuum. Since there were no extant documents from Old Testament times which even mentioned Israel, it was only through surviving fragments of information in Classical sources that it was possible to

3

judge the historicity of any biblical data before the rise
of the Persian Empire (sixth century B.C.). It was, accordingly, only natural to make use of analogies drawn
from ancient and modern times in order to fill this yawn-
ing void.

A few illustrations of the past use of analogy in biblical
research must suffice. While it is true that the first "patch-
work" explanation of the origin of the Pentateuch was
based entirely on the occurrence of different divine ap-
pellations (*Yahweh* and *Elohim*) in passages which
seemed to be somewhat parallel in content, it is still true
that a strong independent stimulus was given to the development of the Documentary Hypothesis by Friedrich
Wolf's famous *Prolegomena to Homer* (1795). The analogy between Homer and Pentateuchal tradition seemed
to be so close in various respects that many doubters
were convinced. Then again, recognition of the antiquity
and uniqueness of Hebrew verse (by Bishop Lowth and
J. G. Herder in the eighteenth century) was greatly ad-
vanced by comparing it with other early literatures such
as Germanic poetry and the works of Homer. Inciden-
tally, this last analogy was correct in essential respects. A
third illustration is Julius Wellhausen's much later comparison of early Israelite modes of life with those of the
Beduin in pre-Islamic or even in modern Arabia, from
which analogies are still being drawn by followers of
Julian Morgenstern and Yehezkiel Kaufmann. In this
area, despite Wellhausen's great authority in Arabic

studies, most analogies have proved to be of little or no value.

Further illustrations of the method in question may be drawn from New Testament studies. Perhaps the earliest and one of the most persistent is the extremely dubious analogy between Apollonius of Tyana, in the late first century A.D., and Christ, in the early second quarter of the same century. This analogy was already drawn by ancient pagan writers and was refuted by such Christian scholars as Eusebius of Caesarea (fourth century A.D.). Eduard Meyer used the rise of Islam and Mormonism to illustrate his interpretation of the beginnings of Christianity. A far better parallel was drawn by Eduard Norden between St. Paul's sermon on Mars' Hill and the Cynic diatribe.

The use of known human analogies and models for better interpretation of less-known phenomena is entirely legitimate in principle, given the well-documented persistence of basic human drives in all kinds of societies, modern primitive, ancient, and modern. But in employing such analogies or models one must be doubly sure that they are really comparable. In other words, one must be sure that cultural and societal factors are duly considered, and that function as well as external form is really comparable. One must also be clear that an analogy or analogies actually point to a stochastic model (i.e., a working hypothesis put into quasi-mathematical form). Above all, then, we should make use of independently convergent lines of evidence which prove that the analogy or model is valid. Without at least two such independent groups of confirmatory evidence, stochastic models seldom amount to more than eventual working hypotheses.

Historical analogy is not simply a type of logical methodology or the use of stochastic models in history, although it includes both. Analogy is basically the application of the principle of resemblance or comparison. All comparisons are in a sense analogies, although, strictly, the term "analogy" is not used in the case of certain clearly demarcated classes of resemblance. In our sense analogy is to be distinguished also from the sense in which it is used in Aristotelian and Scholastic logic where it refers to comparison of words, objects, and ideas, culminating in the *analogia entis*, the analogy of being, employed in scholastic theology as one of the principal arguments for the existence of God. In our day analogy must be differentiated from extrapolation, interpolation, and *metabasis eis allo genos*. Extrapolation is the extension of an equation or curve beyond the actually observable parts of that equation or curve. This is virtually the same as scientific prediction. The two are based on the same mathematical principle, irrespective of the field in which they are applied and of the number of dimensions involved. (It has been argued that prediction works on a three-dimensional level, while extrapolation works in two dimensions, but this is a superficial distinction.) Interpolation is the reconstruction of the section between two given sections of an equation or curve. A comparison drawn between two totally unrelated fields is called by logicians *metabasis eis allo genos*, that is, a transition to a different form of discourse or a different kind of being or existence.

Analogy was first used in a proto-logical or empirico-logical way by primitive man,[1] but has been used on a logical level since Plato and Aristotle. To survey the history of the application of this principle is to discover some of the weaknesses and dangers inherent in its misuse. In the last century analogy played a vital role in the development of the doctrine of evolution, which arose as a shift from what was called homology. Homology was the recognition and study of homologues or counterparts in the structure of vertebrates, and, as a science, enabled biologists and anatomists as early as the seventeenth century to compare skeletal parts of animals. For a long time, and often with little logical or experimental basis, the theory of evolution was developed simply by drawing analogies through homology. In the late 1920's and early 1930's Russian scientists believed that they had discovered a new kind of radiation originating in cell division, which they termed "mitogenetic radiation." An international congress was held on the subject in 1935,

---

[1] It is still so used in the process of intuition. Most intuitions arise from the unconscious application of analogy to basic knowledge existing more or less subconsciously in a person's mind. The novelty of the analogy forces it into the consciousness.

but now the theory has been abandoned by all except possibly a few intractable East European scientists. The reason is simple: the theory was developed on the analogy of the fission of physical atoms and molecules, and never had any experimental basis. Earlier, in the world of physics, "N-rays" had been similarly imagined on the analogy of light. Prosper-René Blondlot of the University of Nancy claimed that he had discovered radiation to which glass was opaque and which passed through substances opaque to light. He further claimed that the diffusion of these "N-rays" was governed by the same laws that govern the diffusion of light. His views were rapidly gaining acceptance when the famous American optical physicist Robert Williams Wood, who was present at one of Blondlot's experiments, removed the lens. The experiment proceeded unaffected and produced the same results. That was the end of N-rays—the analogy had proved worthless.

Today's scientists present us with many analogies which may be pedagogically valuable, but which certainly are not scientific. For example, Fred Hoyle, of the University of Cambridge, in an address arguing for a steady-state universe rather than an expanding universe, drew an analogy between stellar population and human or animal population—a quite unscientific analogy, for the two have no common properties. (This is not to deny that such a comparison may be illuminating for the layman.)

Scientists have used a variety of analogies to describe the universe. There are many who talk of a mechanistic universe, perfectly coordinated, and set this up as the final solution to metaphysical problems. But the theory is based only on analogy and cannot be demonstrated. Other scientists argue in favor of a universe of chance which works on the basis of statistics, but this is no less arbitrary. A third scheme is that of Teilhard de Chardin, who depicts a universe built on the analogy of living, thinking beings, where the outer aspect of the space-time continuum is energy and the inner side is thought—an analogy so vague that it is not susceptible of either proof or disproof. Such analogies are of no value except as entertaining speculations.

Modern philosophers are roughly clustered around what may be called the Hegelian axis and the Kantian axis. The first group lays great stress on analogy, and employs all kinds, drawing on both the physical and biological sciences. Most Kantians are strongly opposed to such use of analogy (Kant himself was keenly aware of the dangers inherent in its misuse), and have even gone so far as to deny the validity of analogy entirely, a fact which has resulted in some very anomalous situations. Ernst Cassirer, one of the great modern neo-Kantian thinkers, had been unwilling to use analogy in any sense until he went to the famous Warburg Institute for the History of Art at Hamburg, when he began to use *metabasis eis allo genos*. And, curiously, he insisted that this was of vital importance while he continued to downgrade the legitimacy of analogy in general. Such hasty acceptance of this form of analogy is typified by a recent proposal of one of our leading theologians, who has seriously suggested the introduction of a new form of theology to be called Cosmological Theology—a theology based on analogies from physics! Here is *metabasis eis allo genos* in an extreme form.

This is enough to indicate the pitfalls which await the person who would use analogy. Yet in spite of these dangers analogy and models are being used constantly by scientists and thinkers in every domain of knowledge, who usually have little or no idea of the limits of application, or of the very applicability, of their methods. It is clear, then, that the next step in the application of logic and philosophy to both natural sciences and social or humanistic studies must be the clarification of concepts in this most important area. It is with great caution that we shall dip into it.

What then is the function of analogy in the study of history? First, the use of a single analogy to solve a historical problem is no more acceptable than induction on the basis of one, two, or three examples. Second, there should be insistence on the restriction of analogies in any given case to a single clear-cut continuum, whatever its nature otherwise, in which there are abundant examples of the analogy. Preferably one would work with all examples that can be found illustrating one case. If all accessible examples support a certain conclusion, their collection still does not constitute proof. Historical proof must come by a wholly different approach to the same material. If *then* there is agreement, the historical analogy may be accepted as either demonstrated, or at least extremely plausible.

In the study of biblical tradition, historical analogy plays a particularly important role, for the Bible is not itself primarily an historical record. It consists of traditions which, although extraordinarily reliable in detail, are often not what the modern historian would consider important. Certain customs and individual events are described at great length because of their subsequent religious significance, but they are of little value in a general historical study. In order to understand the biblical tradition historically, historical analogy must be employed. This has always been true. A study of the historiography of Israel consists largely in the application of different philological approaches and historical analogies to the tradition of Israel as preserved in the Old Testament.

Fortunately, a science of archaeology is now emerging which compensates for many of the deficiencies of historical analogy and carries us much farther in some directions. As early as the 1830's and 1840's, Egyptology became an organized discipline, and during the next three decades, Assyriology rapidly caught up with it and even outstripped it in significance for biblical re-

search. By the 1930's our new knowledge of the ancient
Near East, matrix of the Bible, had become so precise
and extensive that it began to revolutionize biblical research. This came about only after most of the new
scripts and languages had been deciphered and analyzed
on a strict grammatical and lexicographical basis. Even
after the contents of documents were digested and presented systematically in handbooks of religion, law and
customs, arts and crafts, history, and philology, very few
scholars were able to digest the whole mass of pertinent
data. Scarcely any archaeologists could read the languages, much less take part in their interpretation. Few
Assyriologists knew much about Egyptology or archaeology, or could master more than a limited number of other
disciplines, and so with each specialist. There was so
little communication between different fields that works
of a combinatory or synthetic nature were generally produced in symposium form, with participating scholars
writing from individual points of view, often presenting
directly conflicting ideas with widely varying degrees of
competence. They could not check one another's results,
and so there was little cross-fertilization. Today this has
changed because there are reliable handbooks of basic
nature which are available to all and there are many
more scholars with a genuine scientific approach to
research in Accadian, Egyptian, and other languages. Induction is all-important for such research. All relevant
words are collected—every relevant example of gram-

matical form, syntax, or style, from all groups of documents, and from myriads of inscriptions in a variety of different but related languages and scripts, covering thousands of years. All this material must be collected and classified in any given field.

What is true of the languages is also true of the artifacts. As recently as 1925 there was almost no light which archaeology in the narrow sense could throw directly on the Old Testament. There was much relevant material, but it had not yet been accurately interpreted, and could not be precisely dated. The remains of constructions and artifacts had still to be gathered into suitably classified bodies of material which could be explained on the basis of their own context, as well as that of their relationship to other bodies of material which had been excavated.

The term "archaeology" is often narrowly restricted to the study of unwritten monuments—ruins of ancient settlements, tools, utensils, pottery, etc. I shall use it here in its broader sense, including all excavated objects, written documents as well as artifacts. The term "biblical archaeology" may be restricted to Palestine, or it may be extended to include anything that illustrates the Bible, however superficially. Accordingly, I shall use the term "biblical archaeology" here to refer to all Bible Lands—from India to Spain, and from southern Russia to South Arabia—and to the whole history of those lands from about 10,000 B.C., or even earlier, to the present time.

The relevance of archaeology in this sense can scarcely

be questioned. According to Hebrew tradition the Patriarchs came from Mesopotamia in the early second
millennium, and kept their connections with Mesopotamia almost unbroken until the end of Old Testament
times. From Palestine the Patriarchs went down to
Egypt. They were in Egypt for centuries before return-
ing to Palestine, where they remained in close contact
with Egypt during subsequent centuries. In Palestine
they were right at the heart of the civilized world, immediate neighbors of the Phoenicians. All trade, all
movements of culture passed through or immediately
outside the borders of Israel. Thus they were heirs of the
whole of ancient Near Eastern culture. It is to be expected, then, that increasing archaeological knowledge
will have a revolutionary effect on earlier views of the
Bible, whether conservative or liberal, based as they
were on almost total ignorance of the world in which the
Old Testament emerged.

I shall now briefly compare some of the traditional
views of a hundred years ago, the critical reactions
against them which arose from a skeptical approach to
biblical tradition, and the modifications demanded by
modern archaeological knowledge. Before the nineteenth century most Jews and Christians believed that
the Pentateuch had been written down in its extant form
by Moses. Many conservative Jews and Christians
thought that Moses had written even the chapter in
Deuteronomy describing his death. They assumed that

before his death God had told him by inspiration what would happen. When critical scholars in the seventeenth and eighteenth centuries, and especially in the nineteenth century, began to study the Pentateuch, they were struck by its composite character. It was obviously not a book that had been written at one time by one man. From the 1870's through the 1890's a brilliant German Semitist, Julius Wellhausen, applied the Hegelian dialectic to biblical history. He tried, by means of Hegelian analogy with pre-Islamic and Islamic Arabia, to build a system for the development of Israel's history, religion, and literature which would fit his critical analysis. Wellhausen's structure was so brilliant and afforded such a simple, apparently uniform interpretation that it was adopted almost universally by liberal Protestant scholars, and even largely by Catholic and Jewish scholars. There were, of course, some exceptions, but in nearly all places where men were thoroughly schooled by learning Hebrew and Greek and absorbing the critical method, they also learned Wellhausenian principles. Unfortunately all of this was developed in the infancy of archaeology, and was of very little value in interpreting history. The conservatives still maintained that the Hebrew Pentateuch went back with virtually no change to the time of Moses, which was then generally supposed to be about 1400 B.C. The liberal critics also maintained that every word of the Pentateuch had been faithfully preserved, but they put the date at which this text was edited and transformed into its present written form nearly a thousand years after Moses, generally in the fifth century B.C. Both views have been found to be equally wrong.

The Wellhausen structure, which divided the Pentateuch into a number of different documents and even attempted to split single verses among three or more different sources, has proved to be an exaggerated system against which many protests have been leveled. Historians of law, for example, have been shocked at the arbitrary treatment of legal material by men who had never been trained as lawyers or as students of the history of law and legal processes. The different attitudes about the prophets are another case in point. Conservatives thought of the prophets' words as consisting mostly of predictions. For Christians, they were predictions of the Messiah and of future history, for the Jews, predictions of future history (including Messianic). Then came the critical scholars of Europe, who held that the prophets usually did not prophesy before the event, and that when the context states otherwise, the text was tampered with by later editors, in post-exilic times. Critical scholars did valuable service in clarifying the role of the prophets as social and religious reformers. This is a very important consideration for the religious and ethical values of the Bible. Some ultra-conservatives do still insist that the prophets were only predicting the future, and were not referring to contemporary social reform.

Sooner or later archaeological reaction was bound to

set in. Just what its course would be obviously depended on the order in which salient discoveries were made—an order often dependent on sheer accident. Thus relatively minor problems were solved a century ago, while some major ones continue to plague us.

In order to provide a few guidelines, we shall mention some of the outstanding archaeological discoveries which have illuminated biblical research. In order of biblical chronology, first comes the excavation of Mari on the Middle Euphrates, about equidistant between Abraham's traditional home at Ur of the Chaldees and Jerusalem. This work was begun by André Parrot in 1933 and is still going on. Next in this order may be placed the excavation of Nuzi near Kirkuk in eastern Mesopotamia, begun in 1925 and continued for years. This area is at the eastern end of the broad region of northern Mesopotamia where the Hebrew Patriarchs were originally at home. We have at least twenty-five thousand tablets, whole and fragmentary, from these two sites, dating from the eighteenth and fifteenth–fourteenth centuries B.C., respectively. These two collections have thrown a flood of light on Patriarchal backgrounds. M. Parrot, curator of Western Asiatic remains at the Louvre, while excavating at Mari, wrote me once that he had not yet found any direct evidence of Abraham himself—but almost. I think I can now prove that Abraham flourished in the late nineteenth century, i.e., in the century before the Mari tablets. The post-Patriarchal age is then brightly lit up by hundreds of fourteenth-century tablets from Tell el-Amarna in Middle Egypt, capital of the famous heretic king, Akhenaten (Amenophis IV). To these tablets have since been added thousands more from Khattusas (Boğazköy), as well as from other sites in Syria and Palestine. At these sites many thousands of tablets have been found which illustrate many aspects of life in the fifteenth–thirteenth centuries. It is difficult today to imagine the bewilderment of Old Testament scholars when the first reports on the Amarna letters began to appear at the end of the eighties. Julius Wellhausen solved the problem by never referring to them. As late as 1932 a standard two-volume history of Israel appeared in print with scarcely a trace of having been influenced by the Amarna finds. Here then there has been a lag of about half a century.

In 1929 the excavation of Ugarit (Ras Shamra), on the coast of northern Syria, was begun by C. F. A. Schaeffer, and still continues. From this extraordinarily rich site there have come a series of fabulous discoveries illuminating the previously little-known civilization of Canaan. The decipherment of a previously unknown Canaanite alphabet, in which a large part of the tablet hoards from Ugarit were written, has restored much of the long lost Canaanite religious poetry from pre-Israelite times. At the same time the new alphabetic texts have added hundreds of "new" words to our Northwest Semitic (Canaanite-Hebrew) vocabulary and have enabled linguists to reconstruct the forgotten grammar and verse style of pre-Mosaic times. A high proportion of the "new" grammatical phenomena turns out to be represented in one or more of the Palestinian dialects reflected in biblical Hebrew. By utilizing the new information we can explain the words and the grammatical construction of hundreds of hitherto obscure verses of biblical poetry, from Genesis to Job. But the initial decipherment in 1931 has been followed by a third of a century—and still most Old Testament scholars think that Ugaritic has nothing to do with their problems! Faced with such paradoxical lags, the student who keeps up with the progress of scholarship in related fields may be inclined to resort to some of St. Jerome's choice expressions with reference to his die-hard opponents!

In recent years many linear inscriptions in our own ancestral alphabet have turned up in Palestine, Phoenicia, and Syria. We can now date them by archaeological context and evolution of script to the very century in most cases, beginning in the seventeenth century B.C. and continuing into the first millennium B.C. From the tenth century B.C. on, we have steadily swelling collections of alphabetic texts in Hebrew-Phoenician script, enabling us to follow the development of the Hebrew language and its dialects from the Proto-Sinaitic inscriptions[2] about 1500 B.C. to New Testament times. None of this was possible in the nineteenth century.

---

[2] See my monograph *The Proto-Sinaitic Inscriptions and Their Decipherment* (Cambridge, Mass., 1966).

And now we have the scrolls from Qumran! Dating from the early third century B.C. to the sixties of the first century A.D., they contain all of Isaiah and substantial parts of Leviticus, I and II Samuel, Psalms, Habakkuk, etc. More important, they contain many thousands of fragments from virtually all the other books of the Old Testament. In all we have fragments of some one hundred fifty biblical manuscripts, at a conservative estimate. Not one of these copies was made after the year A.D. 68/69, so they average about a millennium older than any Hebrew biblical text of more than a few lines known to exist anywhere in 1947. These fragments are in different textual recensions, which sometimes differ considerably. With the aid of the already well-known ancient translations, especially the Greek (LXX), translated from Hebrew between *ca.* 275 and 100 B.C., we can often restore an earlier form of the Hebrew biblical text. The restored text is often longer than any previously known text, and the details thus recovered sometimes possess great historical importance, as we shall see in Chapters II and III.

Among the new Hebrew recensions of Samuel, to be published by F. M. Cross, Jr., is one which closely resembles the Greek translation of the LXX. The old problem whether the Septuagint or the extant Hebrew preserves a better text is settled in favor of the roughly equal reliability of both texts. Divergences in the Septuagint are seldom the result of mistakes in the Greek text after it began its own independent existence, but more often reflect different Hebrew recensions and misunderstanding of the Hebrew original by Jewish scribes working in Egypt.

Already in use was a form of the text which was virtually identical with the extant Hebrew Bible. This accuracy of transmission through some sixteen hundred years of copying by hand speaks volumes for the care taken by the scribes. Since no manuscript of the Bible which was inaccurate was supposed to be kept in the Synagogue, a scribe who wanted steady employment naturally had to make accurate copies.

Other texts are almost identical with the supposed prototype of the Greek translation. Still others are intermediate, and some reflect an "Old Palestinian" recension which seems to be the prototype of the later "Lucianic" text. This recension contains important historical data, otherwise lost.

II

The Story of Abraham
in the Light of
New Archaeological Data[1]

W HEN SCHOLARS CONSIDER THE STORIES OF
Abraham in the light of archaeology, they en-
counter some of the most difficult problems in the interpretation of biblical tradition. The stories of the Patriarchs, Abraham, Isaac, and Jacob, are told in the Book of
Genesis, and date in their extant written form to the
tenth–seventh centuries B.C. The stories about Abraham,
in Chapters 12 to 25, compose perhaps one of the most
homogeneous blocks of material from the pre-Mosaic
age, i.e., the age of Hebrew beginnings. Until quite
recently it was not possible to check their historical

[1] Cf. *Bulletin of the American Schools of Oriental Research*, No. 163
(1961), 36–54.

basis or authenticity, especially in the case of Abraham. There simply was not enough evidence, and therefore it was possible for scholars to hold almost any conceivable view.

For example, a majority of university-trained biblical scholars have denied the historicity of the Patriarchal narratives, following the dominant Wellhausen school. This school regarded the Patriarchal narratives as consisting almost entirely of "retrojection" from the time of the prophets and kings of Israel, that is, stories that were first told in Israel and Judah between the tenth century B.C. and the Exile (587 B.C.). But Assyriologists since the 1890's and field archaeologists since the 1920's have been pointing out that such retrojection did not harmonize with the increasing number of documentary and archaeological parallels which were coming to light. From these facts it appeared that there might be more basis to these very ancient stories than was commonly believed. But the dissenters were drowned out—and correctly so, in a sense, because they really did not have enough evidence. They found sporadic parallels, sporadic occurrences of very early personal names, and the like, but their evidence was not at all conclusive.

In 1925 excavations were undertaken at Nuzi (see Chapter I). There archaeologists found villas belonging to wealthy property owners of the fifteenth–fourteenth centuries B.C. Among the many thousands of economic and legal texts belonging to the mixed Horite (Hurrian) and Semitic civilization of Nuzi—like the mixed background of the Patriarchs—were found a good many parallels to episodes and allusions in the Patriarchal narratives.

For instance, Genesis 15 says, in passing, that Abraham had no son to be his heir. Instead, his heir was a certain Eliezer of Damascus. Then Isaac is born, and we hear nothing more of Eliezer. Just what does this mean? Before 1925 no one had any idea, because there is no motivation and no explanation; the text simply states, in passing, that Abraham's heir was Eliezer of Damascus. In later Judaism there is no evidence for adoption. But it is now known that in the mixed Hurro-Semitic civilization reflected by the Nuzi texts the practice was widespread of adopting a moneylender as a means of giving the adopted party security for a loan. If the borrower should die, the moneylender would inherit his property. In other words, the Nuzi texts reflect a fixed tradition that family property was not to be alienated, so that if one needed to borrow money one had to adopt a moneylender in order to use property as security. This sort of legal fiction, i.e., a practice which becomes necessary although not directly in accord with legal tradition, is easily paralleled. A good illustration from Jewish law of the New Testament period and later is the *prozbul*, a stipulation that the Sabbatical law of release from debt would not apply in a given case, which circumvented a legal situation that had made economic activity almost impossible.

In the story of Jacob's escape from Laban, Laban's younger daughter Rachel took her father's gods along with her and hid them in the saddle of the beast she was riding. That has always been a puzzle. Why did she take her father's gods with her? [2] The Nuzi texts show that in case there was doubt about the inheritance, the person who had possession of the father's god(s), that is, of the ancestral divinities, would inherit. It is, therefore, obvious that Rachel wanted to assure her inheritance and accordingly stole the "god(s)."

These are only two of at least a score of unmotivated episodes in the Patriarchal narratives which have recently acquired meaning in archaic customary law. These episodes were remembered because, in the case of Eliezer, the succession of Isaac was very important to later Israelite religious tradition, even though the allusion was no longer understood. The story of Rachel was remembered for similar reasons, including the detail of the theft of her father's god(s). Such stories and many others—stories that have no parallels in the Mosaic tradition or in later Israel—actually do contain correct reminiscences of the Bronze Age.

Every year, on the average, we find a new parallel or parallels among the personal and place names from the

[2] Whether it was one god or more we do not know, because the Hebrew term, *teraphim*, has a rather general application to pagan abominations. The Israelites recognized, of course, that their ancestors had worshipped other gods when they lived beyond the river (the Euphrates) in Mesopotamia and when they lived in Egypt. This is explicitly stated in Joshua 24.

first half of the second millennium B.C. (the Middle
Bronze Age), to similar data in the Patriarchal narratives. Mari and Ugarit have provided explanations or
illustrations of many rare words and expressions in Patriarchal and Mosaic tradition.

But still this is only the beginning. When Abraham
lived and how he made a living are questions which have
lacked any clear answer. There were times, beginning
about 1917, when I thought that I had the answer. But
each answer was premature. Every time advances were
made, but no convincing solution was available. Just
who was Abraham? Who were the Hebrews? Why is
Abraham explicitly called a Hebrew in Genesis 14:13, a
section dealing with the enigmatic campaign of the four
kings of the East against southern Palestine and the
desert south of Palestine? Why were the Mesopotamian
kings spending their time in such wretchedly poor areas?

In the nineteenth century and even quite recently
most trained scholars said that Genesis 14 must be apoc-
ryphal, without any historical basis. Yet Genesis 14 contains so many archaisms in language, in personal and
place names, etc., that it has been long impossible for a
serious scholar to deny that its source material must go
back to early times. My own attitude toward the historicity of the chapter has oscillated over the decades,
but has tended to grow more conservative as new material turns up to elucidate this or that obscurity. But
Genesis 14 is still something of a riddle, though its proper

names have nearly all been explained. However, the historical situation of the chapter has remained obscure. I think this can now be cleared up in part.

The personality of Abraham is in some ways easier to understand than that of any other figure in early Israelite tradition. It is quite clear today that there was nothing in the life of the prophets and kings of Israel in the first millennium B.C. which might furnish a basis for fabricating such stories. Since the discoveries at Nuzi and Mari, supplemented by pertinent finds in Babylonia and Egypt, it has become certain that the customary law and mode of life presupposed by the story of Abraham, as well as by the stories of the other Patriarchs, are not fabrications of a late date—they go back to very early times.

E. A. Speiser and F. M. Cross, Jr.,[3] have pointed out that the religious traditions in the stories of Abraham are also very ancient. I was rather slow in coming around to this point of view. In fact, it was not until recently, in preparing a lecture on the sacrifice of Isaac, that I accepted Speiser's position. I now recognize that Speiser and Cross are right; the religious traditions in the story of Abraham are just as archaic as the customary law and the onomastics (study of names). However, not everything about them is necessarily ancient, because all these

[3] See especially E. A. Speiser (ed. and tr.), *Genesis* [W. F. Albright and D. N. Freedman (eds.), *The Anchor Bible*] Vol. I (Garden City, 1964) and F. M. Cross, Jr., *Harvard Theological Review*, LV (1962), 225–59.

stories have passed through long oral transmission. The place in life, or *Sitz im Leben,* as German biblical scholars call it, of this oral tradition has been very obscure. It can now be clarified, as will be seen later.

But the stories of Abraham still did not fit into a recognizable societal pattern. In Genesis 20:1 we read: "And Abraham went from there to the South [the so-called Negev in the south of Western Palestine] and he spent his time between Kadesh Barnea [two well-watered oases only a few miles apart] and the Wall [Shur, the Wall of the Prince, near the Suez Canal line between Egypt and Sinai], while he was an alien resident of Gerar." Gerar was a city at the northern edge of the desert southeast of Gaza, and is identified with modern Tell Abu Hureirah, which contains the remains of a town that covered a considerable area, whose *floruit* dates precisely to the period between 2000 and 1500 B.C.; the only possible explanation for such a large city at this location is that it served as a caravan base at the northern edge of the desert.

Beginning in 1952, Nelson Glueck has spent parts of many summers exploring the Negev of Israel. The most extraordinary result of his explorations has been the discovery of several hundred settlements, some small and some fairly extensive, showing a remarkably homogeneous culture. There is evidence of seasonal occupation in houses, which are usually circular, built with stone foundations and superstructure. They were probably somewhat like the dome-shaped, mud-brick houses of the villagers in Syria and Mesopotamia. But in the Negev there is a good supply of stone, whereas clay for mud brick is not easy to find. Glueck also found many pits which served as water holes or primitive cisterns. In the early second millennium B.C. men had not yet discovered how to conserve water by digging or building cisterns covered with watertight plaster made with slaked lime. Such cisterns were not to be constructed until the last centuries of the second millennium B.C., long after the Patriarchal Age.

To return to the Negev, what are we to make of all these settlements with extremely homogeneous pottery, dating from the twentieth and nineteenth centuries B.C.? In addition, there was seasonal occupation in the valleys or wadis and along the caravan routes of the Negev. The implication of this evidence can be grasped when it is realized that in most other settlements there is no other pottery from any period except the Nabatean-Byzantine, when the Negev was criss-crossed by trade routes. The earliest pottery found in the northern Negev dates from the late fourth millennium B.C. Around Beersheba one finds pottery of other periods as well. But farther south, Glueck found no pre-Nabatean pottery except that of the Middle Bronze I period. For considerably more than a thousand years before and fifteen hundred to two thousand years afterward, there are no remains of pottery or settlements in the southern Negev.

The large number of stone settlements with potsherds scattered over each site makes it obvious that we are dealing with sedentary occupation. Presumably it was seasonal occupation, because of the lack of water during the summer and autumn. However, seasonal residents planted crops, terraced the sides of the wadis, and deflected flash floods into prepared fields which were surrounded with banks to enable water to settle and gradually sink into the ground, thus permitting crops of grain and vegetables to be planted and harvested after winters of normal, though scanty, rainfall (three inches a year or less).

In 1956–57, during the Israeli invasion of Sinai, Nelson Glueck's former assistant Beno Rothenberg crossed over into Sinai proper with the Israeli archaeologists who were exploring the Egyptian side. Around Kadesh Barnea they found over half as many sites of Middle Bronze I as they found from all other periods together. The other periods represented in the area were Late Chalcolithic, Early Bronze, Iron Age, Nabatean, Roman, and Byzantine. There was no pottery from the Islamic period because by then camels had long since come into exclusive use as caravan animals. Pottery is not used by camel nomads for the simple reason that even the hardest pottery, packed in sacking, cannot stand much jouncing on camel back without being broken. So, pottery is found only rarely around medieval or modern Arab encampments, but it does occur at donkey caravan stations, because donkeys walk at a very even pace, raising their hooves no more than absolutely necessary.

In my opinion the puzzling Middle Bronze I settlements in the Negev and farther south along ancient caravan routes in Sinai, can only be understood as serving donkey caravans. In the first place, there is a whole series of settlements of the period, with the same type of house construction and the same indications of seasonal planting, along the old caravan routes in north-central Sinai. Rothenberg, Aharoni, and others found Middle Bronze I pottery even in the heart of this arid desert along the main caravan routes to Egypt. No other pottery at all from any period was found—only pottery of the middle twentieth–nineteenth century B.C.! How can this strange situation be explained?

When Beno Rothenberg's book *The Wilderness of God* appeared in 1961, describing his explorations in Sinai with illustrations of the pottery and with descriptions and plans of the sites where it was found, I realized that the anomalous situation could be explained only by donkey caravan trade. Desert donkeys need water every two or three days, whereas unspoiled desert camels can last a week or longer without water. Camels from Egypt and Palestine prefer water every day or two, and donkeys insist on water at least once a day. Desert donkeys and camels are hardier. Besides, donkeys require fodder or grain like horses, whereas camels can eat a great many desert plants which horses and donkeys cannot

eat. Therefore, donkey caravans had to be supplied with
food along the route, wherever possible. In areas where
no natural fodder was available and transportation costs
were prohibitive, it was necessary to grow all possible
fodder and collect water along donkey caravan routes.

But there is much more evidence for our contention
—a wealth of information from cuneiform and Egyptian
inscriptions, especially Old Assyrian and Egyptian texts
from the very nineteenth century B.C. to which most of
this pottery belongs. They contain details of all kinds
about caravans in northern Mesopotamia and Anatolia,
on the one hand, and in Sinai, Egypt, and Nubia, on the
other hand. In Ankara (1956) I had the opportunity to
spend a good deal of time going over still unpublished
Old Assyrian tablets from Cappadocia with Professor
Kemal Balkan of the University of Ankara, a specialist
on these documents. Nearly all the tablets come from
the nineteenth century B.C. Adding this material and
subsequently discovered tablets to the already published
archival material, we have a vast store of data on donkey
caravaneering in the nineteenth century B.C. These caravans traveled back and forth between Assur, capital of
Assyria (which was their base), and the Assyrian trading
colonies in the region east, southeast, and south of Ankara, which was then the heart of civilized Anatolia. The
donkeys were usually "black" donkeys. These were large
dark-brown animals which could carry an average of
between 150 and 200 pounds of weight all day over

mountain trails. Such donkeys are still found in remote areas in Anatolia, the Aegean, and Syria; they were formerly called "Damascus donkeys."

The Egyptian documents come mostly from Sinai and Nubia; they also date mostly from the nineteenth century b.c.; they state that there were from three hundred to one thousand donkeys in each caravan. These were official government caravans. The size of the Old Assyrian caravans in Anatolia is not known, but there must easily have been up to several thousand beasts in a caravan and seldom fewer than several hundred. The Mari tablets of the following century mention an expedition of three thousand donkeys. The Egyptian caravan donkeys were light gray with brownish patches, as we know from several paintings. The accumulation of corroboratory details makes it certain that there were donkey caravans all over the Near East at that time. This was also a period when the Egyptian empire extended from the Sudan into Syria, and when the commercial expansion of Mesopotamia reached its peak. Hundreds of thousands of donkeys must have been required for the innumerable caravans of the age.

Commerce was already well developed under the kings of the dynasty of Accad, which formed the first large, well-organized empire in ancient history. There were epics handed down by word of mouth and then put into writing in the archaic Accadian sometimes called the Hymnal-Epic dialect, going back to the period

of Sargon and Naram-Sin of Accad, about the twenty-
third century B.C. The first tablet of the great Sargon
Epic, for example, which survives in copies from different places in Western Asia and Egypt, relates that the
official representative of the merchants' guild com-
plained to the king about a certain ruler of Burshakhan-
da, said to be 840 travel hours (420 double hours) dis-
tant. This king in central Anatolia was, they reported,
preventing them from carrying on their normal mercan-
tile activities. It is known from this epic, handed down
by word of mouth from the end of the third millennium
and written down no later than the eighteenth century
B.C., that merchant caravans already were very important. But the empire of the third dynasty of Ur, the
home of Abraham, possessed an even greater commercial
organization. From it there survive scores of thousands
of tablets which give detailed records of government
and private business operations, and demonstrate that
an elaborate system of double-entry bookkeeping existed
some thirty-five hundred years before the time when,
according to many reference books, double-entry bookkeeping is supposed to have been introduced for the first
time. Babylonian accounting was not identical with modern double-entry bookkeeping, but the principle is the
same—two sets of books by which it was possible to
control or check details.

Ur was the capital of a commercial empire that con-
trolled all Mesopotamia, extended into Anatolia, and

even had agents and representatives in Phoenicia, as has recently been discovered. Moreover, the empire sent fleets overseas to Egypt (Makkan) by way of South Arabia, and to India (Meluhha).[4] This great commercial empire, founded by the kings of Ur about a century after the fall of Accad, came to an end about the middle of the twentieth century (*ca.* 1955 B.C.).[5]

Immediately after receiving Rothenberg's volume in June, 1961, I suddenly realized that all the places where Abraham is said to have resided were caravan centers or stations. Ur has been mentioned above. Harran in northwestern Mesopotamia (now in Turkey, a short distance north of the Syrian border) was perhaps founded by the kings of Ur III, since the same Sumerian moon-god was their patron deity, and it has a name meaning "caravan town" in Sumerian. It was a major caravan center in the nineteenth and eighteenth centuries B.C., as we know from both the Cappadocian and the Mari tablets, as well as from an Old Babylonian itinerary. Ur and Harran were the southern and northern ends of a most important trade route up the Euphrates and Balikh rivers in Mesopotamia. Abraham

[4] Some of these discoveries are very recent and remain to be developed in detail before they can be accepted by all scholars, but there is no longer any doubt about the general picture. I. J. Gelb of Chicago has done important work on collecting the personal and place names of Ur III, so we now have a large number of names of places from all over southwestern Asia with which the merchants of Ur traded.

[5] In spite of loud and influential contrary voices, the low chronology is virtually certain; the new evidence accumulated during the past few years places it beyond any reasonable doubt.

may have moved on westward into Syria and Palestine in order to take advantage of the rapidly expanding caravan trade between Egypt and Mesopotamia. He subsequently moved to a new axis between Damascus and Egypt. Damascus is explicitly mentioned in Genesis, and Eliezer, who is said to have come from Damascus, presumably was his financial backer, and, as such, his adopted heir (see above). Among other places with which Abraham is connected by tradition are caravan bases such as Shechem, modern Balatah, at the entrance to a vitally important pass on the watershed ridge road which was then the chief caravan route between Galilee and Sinai. Donkeys could not carry loads across the sands of northern Sinai. They were therefore limited to north-central Sinai, where the surface is hard and strewn with flints, which do not bother donkeys' hooves but can cut the camels' soft pads to ribbons.[6]

Shechem was occupied during the Middle Bronze I period, as G. E. Wright's deep excavations have shown. Deposits from this period are so far down below the top of the mound that no extensive excavation of the level has yet been undertaken.

Bethel lies on the watershed ridge road still farther south. Excavations have been carried on by J. L. Kelso

[6] There is no evidence for the domestication of camels, let alone their use in caravans, before the twelfth century B.C. That camels were kept by some early nomads as sources of food and cloth is likely enough, since they could support nomad life in all but the most arid regions of Arabia.

and the author. The first general occupation of Bethel was in exactly the same period. The pottery from Bethel is identical in type with the pottery which Nelson Glueck found at the sites in Transjordan and the Negev.

The ruins of ancient Hebron are buried deep under modern Hebron, so excavations have so far been undertaken only on the rocky hill of Jebel er-Rumeideh, overlooking the site. Here some remains of Middle Bronze I were found in Philip Hammond's 1965 campaign. In Islamic times Hebron was a great caravan center, and we may assume that this was also true earlier. Gerar has already been mentioned; here caravans coming southward from the coastal plain and down the watershed ridge into the Negev, converged into the old donkey caravan routes across north-central Sinai, marked by settlements strewn with pottery of the Middle Bronze I period.

But who is to tell us that we are not dealing with a series of coincidences? Here we need to bear in mind the discussion of analogy presented in the first lecture. We must have a number of analogies to prove the correctness or applicability of a given model. Our first analogy correlates surface finds along caravan routes of Middle Bronze I with the contemporary donkey caravans which are now so well known from Egyptian stone monuments and Mesopotamian clay tablets. It is hard to see how such an analogy can be completely coincidental. But we have a second, independent analogy be-

tween donkey caravan stations and places mentioned in
the accounts of Abraham's wanderings. Note that only
places are mentioned which are known to have been
important in the donkey caravan trade of that age—Ur,
Harran, Damascus, the watershed ridge of western Palestine, the Negev, and Egypt. Are we here dealing only
with accidental coincidences?

A third series of coincidences appears in passages
from the Abraham narrative in Genesis which can refer
only to caravan trade: Genesis 20:1 (journeys back and
forth between Palestine and Egypt while the Patriarch
lived in a caravan base); Genesis 13:1 ff. (where his
caravan stages are explicitly mentioned); Genesis 15:2 f.
(where his Damascene outfitter is mentioned by name);
Genesis 14:15 (note his "318" armed retainers, necessary
to defend caravans against bandits and nomad raiders).[7]

A fourth independent coincidence is found in Genesis
14:14, where the Patriarch is called "Abram the Hebrew." Now, as I demonstrate elsewhere in detail,[8] the
word 'Apiru/'Abiru (whence 'Ivri) means precisely
"donkey caravaneer." In later times the Hebrews were

[7] In the Amarna tablets (fourteenth century) the king of Hazor writes
in perfectly good archaic Hebrew, "My donkey caravan has escaped.
It is safe" (Amarna, No. 227). Caravans did not always escape intact.
They were frequently raided and robbed (e.g., Amarna, No. 287),
so that the donkey drivers had to be fighting men as well. Later, when
donkey caravans went out of use except on a small scale, the donkey
drivers' descendants often became *condottieri*, or freebooters.

[8] See Chapter II of my forthcoming volume of Jordan Lectures, *Ca-
naan, Phoenicia and Israel: An Historical Analysis of Two Contrasting
Faiths*, soon to be published by the Athlone Press (University of
London).

forced to abandon donkey caravaneering, and turned to other pursuits, so the original sense was forgotten.

The old story of odd and prime numbers is familiar. One can "prove" by a very inadequate induction that odd numbers and prime numbers are identical. One is odd and prime; three is odd and prime; five is odd and prime; seven is odd and prime: four examples, no exceptions. But when we reach nine and fifteen, which are odd but not prime, we see that the "analogy" is quite erroneous. However, in the case of Abraham's occupation we have not one little group of four items where the nature of mathematics is rudely disregarded, but a series of independent analogies or "models," each supported by many relevant, but distinct, items.

It has been clear for some time that the 'Apiru of the fifteenth–twelfth centuries B.C. were stateless people. For example, their personal names often belong to languages foreign to the area where the 'Apiru are found. There are Elamite names, Babylonian names, Northwest Semitic names, even Hittite and Hurrian names. In earlier times the 'Apiru were mostly semi-nomadic groups in northwestern Mesopotamia, around Harran and Nahor (Nakhur) of Patriarchal fame, as well as in southern Armenia. They were divided into tribes grouped into larger aggregations called, respectively, "Sons of the South" (*Bānu Yamīna*=Benjamin) and "Sons of the North (*Bānu Sim'al*). Much clarification of Hebrew prehistory is to be expected from still unpublished tablets and studies.

The original meaning of 'Apiru as "Dusty One(s)" was pointed out a number of years ago by E. Dhorme and R. Borger. This designation has excellent analogies in the designation of "grooms" (humble men who took care of chariot horses and chariots, running in the dust behind their masters) as LÚ.SAKHARA, "Dusty Ones." Similarly, the hucksters who walked behind their mules as they peddled their goods in medieval England were called by the Anglo-Norman nickname "pie-powders" (Old French *pieds poudres,* "dusty feet"). The term "Dusty Ones" was singularly appropriate for donkey caravaneers, trudging in the middle or behind long lines of loaded donkeys!

When, after the eighteenth century B.C., the donkey caravaneers were forced into other occupations by the increasing use of mules and wagons, the term 'Apiru became 'Abiru, "One from Beyond" (a river or boundary), by a common phonetic change and a popular etymology. This form and meaning were remembered by later Israelites; outside the Bible it appears for the first certain time in cuneiform tablets of the twelfth–eleventh centuries B.C. And yet we still have an echo of the old tradition in Genesis 18:27, where Abraham is represented as saying "I am (only) dirt and fine dust." [9]

[9] Hebrew *'afar wa'efer* does not really mean "dust and ashes"; the expression was long ago identified by Hugo Winckler with Amarna *'aparu/epru* (this Accadian word for "dust" is the source of Hebrew *'efer*). I owe the biblical reference to Dr. M. Gertner of London.

There are, of course, other areas of Patriarchal tradition which have been illuminated by archaeological discovery. Detailed discussion of them must await the future.[10]

---

[10] See also my forthcoming volume of Jordan Lectures on Canaan, Phoenicia and Israel, Chapter II.

III

Reconstructing Samuel's Role in History[1]

IN RECONSTRUCTING WHAT APPEARS TO BE THE historical role of Samuel, historical analogy must play a very important part. While archaeology is also important, its bearing is not nearly so direct in assessing the place of Samuel as in determining Abraham's historical role, which we have just discussed. With Samuel we face a radically different series of problems. Again, how-

[1] My point of view was first presented as the Goldenson Lecture for 1961, entitled *Samuel and the Beginnings of the Prophetic Movement* (Cincinnati, 1961). It was not until early the same year that I read William Sargant's brilliant book *The Battle for the Mind* (New York, 1957) in its 1961 Penguin edition. In this connection I wish to express my gratitude to my research assistant in 1958–59, Emunah Finkelstein (now Mrs. E. Katzenstein) for her aid in working out other details of the Samuel problem.

ever, recently recovered finds in Qumran and elsewhere
are of vital significance.

In the Bible Samuel appears almost exclusively in the
first chapters of I Samuel—and the genealogical lists of
I Chronicles. There are only three additional references
to him in the Old Testament, and only one of them has
independent historical significance. Modern historians
of Israel have been extremely cautious in trying to ap-
praise Samuel's historical role. For example, the distinguished German historian Martin Noth of Bonn in his
book *The History of Israel* mentions Samuel only in
passing. John Bright's admirable book *A History of
Israel* (1959) shows commendable caution in dealing
with such an enigmatic figure. For my own part, before
1961 I was also unable to understand the historical role
of Samuel, so I preferred not to mention him except in-
cidentally. The primary cause of confusion was that the
Samuel tradition is heterogeneous in character and there
are vitally significant contradictions in it.

There are four different types of contradiction which
I shall describe briefly. According to a tradition which
appears in I Samuel 1:1, Samuel was a member of the
tribe of Ephraim and the clan of Zuph. But in the Chron-
icler's genealogy, I Chronicles 6:16–43, we find Samuel
listed as a member of a family of Levitic singers, i.e., he
belonged to the tribe of Levi and was a member of the
guild of singers within this tribe. Which view is correct?

We are told that Samuel was, toward the end of his

career, a little-known diviner, so obscure that Saul had to ask his servant who Samuel was, even though the latter lived within a few hours' walk from Saul's home (I Samuel 9:6 ff.). On the other hand, it is reported that Samuel was judge over all Israel and that he turned over his office to his two sons when he retired (I Samuel 7:15 ff.; 8:1 ff.). What were the facts?

Then again, Samuel is said to have defeated the Philistines in a pitched battle and to have freed Israel from their domination "all his days" (I Samuel 7:3–14). But other texts (I Samuel 10:5; 13:3, etc.) say that Israel was under Philistine domination to the end of Samuel's active life as judge of Israel. Which account is correct?

A fourth type of contradiction appears in the reports (I Samuel 8:16 ff., etc.) that Samuel was strongly opposed to the establishment of a monarchy. Elsewhere it is stated that Samuel favored it (I Samuel 9:17 ff., etc.). Which view is right?

Modern scholars, beginning especially with Julius Wellhausen, have tried to distribute the narratives of Samuel among different documentary sources. In Genesis this can be done to a certain extent, thanks to the two divine names, *Yahweh* and *Elohim*. However, in the Book of Samuel there are no such concrete criteria of form, so that scholars who try to use the divergent traditions about Samuel's role as a means of differentiating documentary sources are soon reduced to speculation. In the absence of clear-cut differences in wording and structured formulas, it is impossible to classify literary sources on the basis of content alone.

The analysis of the Hebrew recensions of I and II Samuel by Frank M. Cross, Jr., as they appear among the sheepskin fragments of Cave IV at Qumran, is at last providing us with a textual basis for the study of Samuel's career.[2] All three Qumran IV scrolls of Samuel agree much more closely with the Greek translation than with the Masoretic Hebrew; the text of the oldest copy is definitely superior to both Greek and Hebrew. Since this early copy is almost certainly older than the Greek translation of Samuel, this situation is not surprising. It must be emphasized that each recension fills out gaps in the other; the original text was, therefore, fuller than either Septuagint or Masoretic Hebrew (the text of our printed Bibles). In other words, the original text of Samuel was longer than any derived recensions, and naturally longer than all modern translations. Where the Greek and Hebrew differ, most apparent recensional variants were already found in the earlier text. Since we find similar indications of a fuller original text in Genesis, Exodus, Numbers, Deuteronomy, Joshua, and Judges, we may be sure that all these books share in the tendency to reduce the original text through copyists' errors, instead of expanding it by editorial glosses. Therefore, it is impossible to carry out any of those close analyses

[2] See F. M. Cross, Jr., *The Ancient Library of Qumran and Modern Biblical Study* (New York, 1958), especially pages 31 ff. and 133 ff.

of the Hebrew text which became so popular in the late nineteenth and early twentieth centuries. The text of the Hebrew Bible was not fixed at such an early date as supposed by most critical scholars, a fact which means that the Masoretic text cannot be used as a basis for the kind of analysis which sometimes divided a single verse among three different sources.

Just what this means in terms of textual criticism is easy to see. Most losses are the result of the repetitive style of oral transmission, where we have statements as to what will occur or instructions about what is to be done, followed by narratives in which the events are narrated as having happened or the instructions are said to have been carried out in detail. In Canaanite (Ugaritic) prospective and narrative epic texts we have similar scribal omissions, which must be restored to their places in both doublets in order to understand the text. In most cases, both in the epics and the Bible, scribal omissions are caused by remembering parallels and omitting words because the scribe was under the impression that he had already written something which he had, in fact, only remembered.

These divergent traditions in Samuel provide material for historical inferences of great significance. Historians are much better off when they can utilize independent reports of actual events than when they must depend on an already canonical tradition, a tradition which has eliminated differences and established a standard account of what took place; for example, there used to be an orthodox American tradition about George Washington. These orthodox traditions commonly grow around important historical figures, but there is no standard tradition of Samuel. Later editors of the Deuteronomic history, which incorporates the books of Deuteronomy, Joshua, Judges, I and II Samuel, I and II Kings, and which was written in its present form either in the late seventh or the early sixth century B.C., obviously made painstaking efforts to keep the old traditions as intact as possible. Where these had been harmonized and reduced to what may be called canonical form in earlier times, as was certainly the case in Joshua, the Deuteronomic editors transmitted the record as they found it. But they found no such harmonized account of Samuel. They may have been quite puzzled as to what role Samuel actually played, but they were careful to preserve the divergent accounts. Thanks to their *pietas,* the historical significance of Samuel can still be seen in the perspective of varying traditions at almost every phase of his career.

By the combined use of archaeological and philological research with the indispensable aid of historical analogy, it is possible, I think, to clarify most of the "contradictions." The first problem is whether Samuel was a layman or a Levite. The Mishnah, which is the oldest of the great depositories of Rabbinic law, dating from the second century A.D., tells us that Samuel was a *nāzîr,* a Nazirite. The term *nāzîr* is an old passive participle meaning etymologically, "one who is vowed." A Nazirite

was typically a person vowed by his parents, before
birth, to the service of God (or the sanctuary); he was
not to shave or cut his hair, nor to touch alcoholic beverages. In the Masoretic Hebrew text we are told that no
razor was to pass over Samuel's head, and the Greek
Bible adds that he was not to drink alcoholic beverages.
Accordingly, it was formerly thought by most scholars
that Samuel was a Nazirite, although later critical scholars rejected this tradition, arguing that there was no
explicit evidence that Samuel was a Nazirite. But now
a Dead Sea Scroll fragment of Samuel already published
by Frank M. Cross, Jr., states explicitly (I Samuel 1:22)
that Samuel's parents were to dedicate him to the service of the sanctuary at Shiloh as a Nazirite forever (nāzîr
'ad 'ôlām).[3] Ben Sira (46:13) states emphatically (ca.
200 B.C.) that Samuel was a nezîr Yahweh, "one vowed
to the Lord." [4]

Samuel was associated with the cult through much of
his life and it is not surprising, therefore, that later
Levitic traditions in Chronicles make him a Levite. We
do not know whether or not he was actually adopted
into the Levitic "tribe," though there is evidence for

[3] See Bulletin of the American Schools of Oriental Research, No. 132
(1953), 15–26.
[4] Thanks to the Hebrew text of Ben Sira (Ecclesiasticus), discovered
by S. Schechter in the Cairo Genizah, and published since 1897, we
now have the text of this book in its original form. That the Hebrew
of the Genizah is indeed original and not a retranslation into Hebrew
in medieval times, has been proved by Y. Yadin's discovery of a manuscript of the book in his excavation of Masada (found in 1964, published in 1965). This manuscript had been written in the early first
century B.C., a century or so after the first composition of the book!

the practice of adoption in early Israel. There is no reason to doubt that later tradition is correct with regard to his function, especially since Israelites of later times could no longer understand how a non-Levite could become a Levite or could serve in the tabernacle. We therefore have a solid basis for explaining the origin of two seemingly so divergent points of view.

In the second place, was Samuel judge of all Israel or only a little-known diviner? We actually have good reason to think that he was both judge and a man of the charismatic gifts associated in Israel with divining. As patron of the ecstatic prophets, to whom I shall turn later, he was a member of their circle, which was intimately bound up with such charismatic functions as divination. When he is called a *rō'eh* or "seer" it does not mean that he was a diviner in the Babylonian or even in the Canaanite sense. In other words, he was not like Balaam, a professional diviner with long training in the complicated "sciences" of divination. Instead, he was associated with the *ḥōzîm* who gave oracles through visions, or in some other simple way accepted by the Israelites. As we have said, he was closely connected with the ecstatic prophets, who were also oracular diviners. Furthermore, he was "a man of God," a prophet (a *nābî*, which means, as we know now, "one called to a vocation").[5]

[5] Both in Old Babylonian and in early Northwest Semitic—the linguistic group to which the Patriarchs belonged—we find the same verb used of "calling," "naming," and "giving of a commission (to a man by a god)." *Nābî* does not mean "speaker," for Moses was *nābî* but

As charismatic leader of Israel, i.e., as a leader who was commonly recognized as having a special gift from God, as a person around whom resistance to the enemy crystallized, as an arbitrator, or as a civic leader, Samuel was also called "judge" (*shôphēṭ*). Samuel remained at the same time, however, a religious leader of Israel, as his public roles are not contradictory. As a charismatic religious leader he may not have been as well known to the ordinary Israelite of his day as he later became when he was a charismatic intertribal arbitrator.

The question whether Samuel triumphed over the Philistines or whether Israel was subject to the Philistines "all his days," can be answered similarly. We know from Assyrian inscriptions of the ninth–seventh centuries B.C., that even the cruel Assyrians repeatedly forgave rebels and restored them to the places they held before their rebellion. It is much easier to rule a people through their own recognized, legitimate ruler, even if he is acknowledged only by a minority, than through a governor or viceroy imposed from outside. So I have no doubt that both traditions are substantially correct. We know that Philistine fortresses were built in different parts of Palestine[6] assuring some kind of control. The

---

not a speaker (in which capacity Aaron took his place). The *nābî* was specially called by God; he was not necessarily a prophet or diviner.
[6] In 1922 and 1933 I directed the excavation of the Philistine fortress at Gibeah (Tell el Ful) from the late eleventh century B.C., and M. Dothan has recently cleared the site of a fortress of the same type at Kadesh Barnea. Other such fortresses seem to be known.

Philistines were probably not interested in setting up
an empire of normal administrative type, but chiefly in
controlling the east–west trade routes between the
Coastal Plain and Ammon on the edge of the desert; and
in order to protect the routes they had to control the
population. One technique they employed was main-
taining a monopoly of iron, as described in I Samuel
13:19–21. The Israelites had to go down to the Philistines
to procure even their iron plow tips and other iron instruments of agriculture, and they were naturally not sold
iron weapons. Though the Philistines had fortresses and
garrisons in Israel in order to defend the principal trade
routes, we may suppose that they generally left Israelite
affairs to Israelite tribal heads and to such recognized
charismatic leaders as Samuel.

Finally, what was the attitude of Samuel toward the
monarchy? In retrospect it seems strange that no one
has quite recognized the actual situation.[7] Titularies
were very important in antiquity, just as they are in
some countries today. In those days titles meant more
than they do today even in title-minded countries, because people now are a little freer from the tyranny of
words than were most people of the ancient Near East.
It is therefore important to note that Saul, the first king
of Israel—using the usual English designation—was,
according to the formula used three times in I Samuel,

[7] A. Alt, M. Noth, and John Bright (especially the latter, *A History of
Israel* (Philadelphia, 1959), 169, have come closest to the view here
stated.

anointed not as *melek*, or king, but as *nāgîd*. In other words, he was not anointed as king at all. David is explicitly said to have been anointed four times as *nāgîd*, but he is never said to have been anointed as *melek*, although that term is elsewhere applied to him. We are told in one passage that Solomon was anointed as *nāgîd*. But the term *melek* early became conventional in the southern kingdom, which had become an hereditary monarchy. However, the northern kingdom remained a quasi-elective monarchy much of the time on a traditionally charismatic basis, as has often been pointed out, and the official term *nāgîd* continued there at least until the time of Baasha. The word *nāgîd* meant "military leader." Scholars have forgotten that in Aramaic dialects of post-Christian times the cognate words *negîdâ* and *nâgôdâ* both meant "leader, commander." In one of the Aramaic treaties from Sefîreh in northern Syria, dating from the middle of the eighth century B.C., the king of Arpad mentions successively, "one of my sons (*bny*), one of my commanders (*ngdy*), or one of my officials (*pqdy*)," so it is quite clear that the term had the same meaning as in later Aramaic dialects. Nevertheless, even such a great scholar as Albrecht Alt tried to explain the term differently. Others have also offered various explanations, such as "a person who announces," Hebrew *higgîd*, "to announce." Here I should simply observe that quite unnecessary confusion is introduced by trying to explain words by etymology instead of from actual usage.

Samuel's action then consisted in helping the Israelites to choose a military leader who would presumably differ from a "judge" in holding a constitutional instead of charismatic office during his lifetime—or possibly for a term of years. There is thus no reason to suppose that Samuel intended to introduce a monarchal system of government into a land which prided itself on having no king but Yahweh.

As an historical analogy one might point out that from 509 B.C. to the Augustan period, the republican Romans were just as bitterly hostile to the establishment of a monarchy as the Israelites were during the three centuries before Saul. Caesar never became king, even though his own name eventually became the title of the emperor of Germany (*kaiser*) and of Russia (*czar*). Even Augustus came in as *princeps* and *imperator*, "commander of the army," not as king. But the title *imperator* came to mean "emperor," and in Israel, under the stress of a continued state of war, the elected military commander eventually developed into a king.

These apparent contradictions can thus be understood and explained, without having recourse either to arbitrary harmonization or to attribution of the conflicting traditions to equally arbitrary sources. In most cases we need a more correct Hebrew text and more evidence as to the meaning of words from early inscriptions. These data are provided by archaeology, which also furnishes the cultural background so necessary for the understanding of Samuel's background. Yet divergences be-

tween the different traditions still exist, and they help
to give us a perspective view of the public role of Samuel
which we could not possibly have if we were limited
only to canonical, standardized tradition that had already been harmonized before our oldest now known
biblical texts.

In a sense, Samuel was the last charismatic leader of
Israel. In his lifetime Israel changed from an amphictyonic confederation of tribes[8] united around the central sanctuary at Shiloh, to an embryonic monarchy.
Significant as this role may have been, Samuel's place in
the spiritual history of Israel was much more important.
In Jeremiah 15:1 we find the prophetic statement,
"Yahweh the Lord said to me (Jeremiah), 'Even if Moses
and Samuel stood before me [as advocates of Israel in
litigation before God, presiding over the divine assem-
bly of angels], I would still not favor this people.' " God
is the supreme judge, and the prophet suggests that even
if Moses *and* Samuel were to stand as advocates before

[8] Following the lead of Albrecht Alt and especially of his pupil Martin
Noth, most scholars now term Israel an amphictyonic confederation,
using the Greek word *amphictyonia*, applied to tribes or towns that
belonged to a league formed around a central sanctuary. There were
many of these leagues in Greece, western Asia Minor, and Italy; they
formed a remarkably close historical analogy to the amphictyonic
confederation of Israel. According to the Wellhausen point of view,
there was no central sanctuary before post-exilic times, when the
Temple in Jerusalem became the only sanctuary accepted by true
Jews. Yet there were many such central sanctuaries in the ancient
Near East, and it would be rather strange if early Israel were an exception. Not only were there central sanctuaries, but there were also
high priests all over the Near East, again unknown to Wellhausen.

the heavenly court, God would still condemn the people
of Israel who had repeatedly disobeyed the terms of
His covenant, thereby incurring its sanctions (i.e., the
curses which were invoked on those who broke the terms
of a treaty).[9]

For the religious background of Samuel we must
stress his connection with Shiloh, where the Tabernacle
had been located for generations. As the center around
which the amphictyonic confederation of twelve tribes
was established, it was vitally important in the religious
as well as the political life of early Israel. We are told in
the plainest language that the Shilonite priesthood,
which seems to have continued in the same family since
the Conquest, had become corrupt. To judge from
Samuel's later career he must have been an extremely
earnest young man from a very devout family. There is,
accordingly, no reason to doubt that as a youth Samuel
had been horrified by the corruption he saw around him
at Shiloh. Furthermore, shortly after the middle of the
eleventh century B.C. the Philistines invaded Israel. In
order to be sure of victory, the Israelites took the Ark
with them to the edge of the low hill country of Ephraim
opposite the Philistine base at Aphek (Ras el-'Ain). In
the ensuing battle the Israelites were defeated and the

[9] See especially the admirable study by Delbert R. Hillers, *Treaty-
Curses and the Old Testament Prophets* (Rome, 1964). Note that
these covenants with God, which appear to have been uniquely Israelite, probably go back to the early caravaneering days of the Hebrews,
when they had to make innumerable treaties and contracts with states,
tribes, suppliers and merchants.

Ark was captured. Since it had proved itself worthless as a palladium, the Philistines allowed it to remain on the frontier between Israel and Philistia during the age of Philistine domination, and it was not brought back to sanctuary in Israel until well along in the reign of David. Presumably many Israelites also had doubts about the Ark, though we have various accounts of its deadly effect on Philistines and Israelites who treated it irreverently. Furthermore, Jeremiah in two different passages tells us that Shiloh had been in ruins since the destruction of the Tabernacle. The Danish excavations at Shiloh, modern Seilun, have proved that Shiloh had indeed been destroyed about the middle of the eleventh century B.C. and that there was scarcely any trace of later occupation until the Persian period, after the time of Jeremiah. This is further supported by statements in one of our oldest psalms, Psalm 78, which dates from the tenth century B.C. and is historically very important, since it preserves a number of early Israelite traditions which we do not find in any other source.[10] Here we are explicitly told not only that the Tabernacle was destroyed but also that its priests were slaughtered. Saul, after quarreling with Samuel, later brought priests to a place called Nob, near Saul's residence in Gibeah, modern Tell el-Ful, not far from Jerusalem. Yet nowhere in the story of Samuel can

---

[10] As emphasized by O. Eissfeldt; see his *Einleitung in das Alte Testament* (Tübingen, 1956), 271 f., and *Das Lied Moses Deuteronomium 32 1–43 und das Lehrgedicht Asaphs Psalm 78 samt einer Analyse der Umgebung des Mose-Liedes* (Berlin, 1958).

we find any indication that he was interested in the re-
establishment of the Tabernacle and its ritual or in the
restoration of the Ark. There is a famous passage in I
Samuel 15 which is quoted from early sources in its
original poetic form:

> Behold, to obey is better than sacrifice,
> To listen than the fat of young lambs.

We find this sentiment echoed again and again in Hosea,
Isaiah, Micah, and Jeremiah. It became a commonplace
among the later prophets, who ascribed only relative
significance to the sacrificial ritual. For them, obedience
to God, behavior in accord with the terms of the Covenant, and kindness to one's neighbor were much more
important than ritual and sacrifice.

No matter where we turn in our examination of I
Samuel, the prophet seems to have broken away from
cultic tradition. For instance, we find the old high places
replacing the central sanctuary. As we have seen, neither
Tabernacle nor Ark seems to have interested the ardent
reformer. Instead of priests we find ecstatic prophets.

In I Samuel 19:20 we read: "And the band of prophets
were in an ecstatic frenzy, and Samuel was presiding
over them." Two different Hebrew words having the
same meaning are here used in order to make it perfectly
clear that when Saul came to the band of prophets,
Samuel was presiding over their dances and ecstatic

music. In two of these stories Saul is said to have been converted by the activity of the prophets and to have become one of them himself. On both occasions the same proverb is quoted, "Is Saul also among the prophets?" In other words, can a man like Saul become a religious ecstatic? Saul was obviously known as big and tough, and certainly not as the kind of man to be expected in a band of prophets.

The prophets appear in I Samuel as groups playing various instruments, dancing and acting like ecstatics. In other words, they worked themselves up into a frenzy under the influence of music and dancing, and then finally went into trances. Saul himself is said to have thrown off his clothing, gone into a trance, and lain naked all night. Today we have a much clearer neuropsychological understanding of this phenomenon, such as is presented in the illuminating analysis by William Sargant in *Battle for the Mind*. Being himself an eminent neuropsychologist, completely opposed to Freudian and other forms of mythopoeic psychoanalysis as well as to the "analytical psychology" of C. G. Jung, he is able to examine their methods, as well as the methods of brainwashing successfully employed by Communists. For our purpose the most instructive part of the book is its survey of the history of revival movements among Protestant bodies, and the technique of individual conversion. Being himself a Wesleyan Methodist, Sargant is in sympathy with what he calls the "spiritual capital" built up by early ecstatic religious movements. And here again I want to illustrate the application of historical analogy.

When people get into a state of acute nervous or mental distress, with the accompanying physiological symptoms such as sweating, rigor of the limbs, and hysteria of various types, it may bring about a complete transformation of the behavior pattern. This phenomenon was first studied systematically in dogs by the Russian psychologist Pavlov, whose pioneer work has been followed by further experimental study of animals and scientific analysis of parallel reactions in human beings. As a result of this research, a good deal is now known about the transformation of behavior patterns. In the past many liberal biblical scholars argued that when it is said of Saul that he received a new heart, it does not mean that he was "converted," but that he was believed to have been changed by some process of sympathetic magic, becoming a different personality from what he had been before. However, this is not magic, but physiology or neuropsychology. The description in I Samuel (not mentioned by Sargant) of the ecstatic prophets, of Samuel's relationship to them, and of Saul's activities in connection with them, is almost identical with descriptions of similar movements in quite recent history. St. Paul was troubled by some of these manifestations, such as "speaking with tongues," although he recognized that they had a place in infant Christianity. When people are profoundly affected mentally and nervously, after subjection to a period of intense pressures, they tend to seek release with the aid of violent rhythmic exercises such as dancing to music.

There would be no Methodism today if it were not for the revival movements inaugurated by Wesley and Whitefield, which continued for generations. There would be no Quakers without the wild meetings of the seventeenth century, in which the Friends built up a vast neuropsychological "capital" and experienced both mass and individual conversions. In early and medieval Christianity there were similar upsurges of ecstaticism, from Pentecost on. A striking parallel in later Judaism is the Hasidic movement, whose "rebs" and "tzadikim" were the despair of all the well-educated orthodox rabbis of the eighteenth century A.D.

In the ecstatic movement in Samuel's time we thus see unmistakable evidence of Samuel's intimate connection with the beginnings of the later Israelite prophetic movement.

Did this new movement create literature of its own, going back to the time of Samuel? In agreement with most scholars I used to think that there was no prophetic literature before the eighth century B.C. Edward Robertson of Manchester had long insisted, with almost no success, that Deuteronomy goes back substantially to Samuel. I cannot accept his specific formulation of the argument, but Deuteronomy is unthinkable apart from the prophetic movement, and the prophets of Israel are equally unthinkable without Samuel. In 1958 Otto Eissfeldt published a monograph in which he contended that the majestic poem in Deuteronomy 32 goes back to Samuel's time.[11] At first I was not unnaturally skeptical. In my book *From the Stone Age to Christianity* (1940) I had held to the usual critical date in the seventh century B.C., though in later editions (1946 on) I changed the date of the poem to the tenth century. But after reconsidering the evolution of poetic style in early Israel, I came to the conclusion that Eissfeldt is correct about the date. On the other hand I cannot agree with his idea that the religion of Samuel was semi-pagan. The exact opposite must be true—that Samuel's religion was ultra-monotheistic, like Deuteronomy 32.

As a result of my own past work (since 1944) and Eissfeldt's discovery, we must now look at early Hebrew poetry from an entirely different point of view. Modern critical scholarship, almost entirely dependent on Wellhausen, had denied the early date of nearly all poetry in the Old Testament. The Psalter was supposed to be the hymnbook of the post-exilic temple or even of the Maccabaean period, although with a few earlier poems. Early poems such as the Song of Miriam (Exodus 15), the Song of Moses (Deuteronomy 32), and the Blessing of Jacob (Genesis 49), were generally referred to post-exilic times or at the earliest to late pre-exilic times.

[11] See n. 10 above.

Only the Song of Deborah and a few fragments were treated as exceptions. In short, these scholars claimed that prose nearly always preceded poetry in Israel, making Israel the only exception to the historical fact, apparently general in the eastern hemisphere, that poetry precedes literary prose. The reason for this priority is simple. Only sung or chanted poetry can survive the vicissitudes of oral transmission. Whether we turn to Greece or Rome; to ancient Arabia, Canaan, Egypt, or Babylonia; to early Romance, Germanic, Slavic, Indian or Chinese literatures, we find that poetry came first, with only apparent exceptions. Israel would accordingly be the only known exception in the Old World, which would be hard to believe for anyone not impervious to rational arguments. And yet, of course, we cannot prove a case like this by a single historical model, even though the model may seem to be valid in all comparable cases.

Fortunately, there is entirely independent evidence. As a result of the discoveries at Ras Shamra (Ugarit), we know the immediate background of early Hebrew poetic language and style (see above, Chapter I). And it is precisely the Mosaic and early post-Mosaic poems of the Bible that almost invariably exhibit style and grammar approaching most closely to corresponding characteristics of such Canaanite mythological poems as "Baal," "Aqhat" (Danel), "Keret," etc., all of which were first put into writing not later than the fourteenth

century B.C. In the Song of Miriam (Exodus 15), which
describes the Exodus in the early thirteenth century
B.C., we find the closest resemblances in style and language. It is quite impossible to maintain seriously today
that the Song of Miriam is post-exilic or even post-
Solomonic. Employing sequence dating, we may pro-
ceed from Canaanite to the earliest Israelite style of
the thirteenth century, then to the manner of the twelfth
and eleventh centuries and finally to the style of the
tenth–eighth centuries.[12]

The chronological shift reminds one of the changing
poetic styles of early Rome, or of Anglo-Saxon literature, which develops from Beowulf to Chaucer with a
changing style which makes it possible to date poems
within comparatively short periods by style and language alone. So there is confirmation of the historical
analogy by the convergence of stylistic criteria and
content of the poems. The argument from the evolution
of Hebrew style agrees with the internal evidence of
date which may be derived from analysis of the content
of these early Hebrew poems. We have, accordingly,
three independent lines of evidence which constitute
as many independent historical analogies: (1) the analogy of other literatures; (2) the analogy of external
form; (3) the analogy between the content of the poems
and external tradition.

[12] For a detailed account see Chapter I of my Jordan Lectures on
Canaan, Phoenicia and Israel.

Another series of historical analogies illustrates the partial replacement of priests by prophets in the religious society of Israel. All the following examples come from the Judeo-Christian continuum and illustrate "the interaction of two distinct elements in periodic tension: an institutionalized hierarchy of religious functionaries and an upsurge of charismatic spiritual leaders." [13] In time the charismatic element became hierarchic, and a new total or partial replacement was needed in order to awaken the dormant consciences of believers and set needed reforms in motion. Examples are too numerous to list; a few will do. Between *ca.* 165 B.C. and A.D. 135, the Pharisees, Essenes and Christians replaced the ancient priests and Levites by laymen, called "teachers," "overseers" and "elders," to pick out a few outstanding designations. Teachers became rabbis, overseers became "bishops," and "elders" became "priests" (*prester* from *presbyter*). From the fourth century A.D. on, the members of monastic orders gradually complemented the older hierarchy, sometimes virtually displacing the "secular" clergy. Priests and monks stood for many centuries in much the same relationship as priests and prophets in pre-exilic Israel. Probably the built-in system of checks and balances that has kept the Catholic Church on an even keel so long also operated in Israel, preventing a collapse of the hierocratic state with the priesthood, as happened at Shiloh. Some of Jeremiah's

[13] Albright, *Samuel and the Beginnings of the Prophetic Movement*, 19.

significance comes from the fact that he was both priest and prophet. In Protestantism we have the replacement of Roman priests by Lutheran and Calvinist "shepherds" (pastors), and in the eighteenth century we find Anglican priests replaced among the Methodists by lay preachers (who soon became ordained "ministers"). About the same time the Hasidic sect of Jewry replaced the educated rabbi by the miracle-working ecstatic "reb" or "tzadik."

We began these lectures by discussing the use of historical analogy and models; we hope that enough examples have been given to demonstrate the utility of these tools for Biblical research. In the absence of direct evidence, the historian must often employ analogy. At the same time, however, we hope that enough has been said to show that analogy may be a useful tool, but it is not a precision instrument. Improper use of models is more dangerous than total neglect of analogy. Yet it is of the highest importance that we do not on that account dismiss this useful and diversified tool as completely worthless.

INDEX